# Really

# ⋀Short W

# North Dartmoor

### Paul White

G000277594

Bossiney Books · Launceston

First published 2005 by
Bossiney Books Ltd, Langore, Launceston, Cornwall PL15 8LD
www.bossineybooks.com

ISBN 1-899383-24-7

**Acknowledgements**
The maps are by Graham Hallowell
Cover design by Heards Design Partnership
Photographs by the author
Printed in Great Britain by R Booth Ltd, Mabe, Cornwall

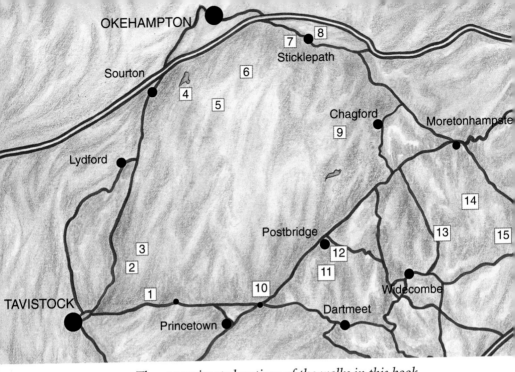

*The approximate locations of the walks in this book*

## Other Bossiney books you may find useful

To understand Dartmoor

*Ancient Dartmoor*
*Medieval Dartmoor*
*The making of modern Dartmoor*
*About Dartmoor*
*Ponies on Dartmoor*
*Supernatural Dartmoor*

Bossiney Walks Books

*Really short walks south Dartmoor (in preparation)*
*Shortish walks on Dartmoor  (5-8km walks)*
*North Dartmoor pub walks (in preparation)*
*South Dartmoor pub walks (7-13km walks)*
*Shortish walks in north Cornwall  (5-8km walks)*
*Shortish walks in north Devon  (5-8km walks)*
*Shortish walks on Exmoor  (5-9km walks)*

# Introduction

The walks in this book are approximately 3-5 km (2-3 miles) in length. Some are easy, others are short but quite challenging, so you may need to be selective. They have been chosen to show you some of the pleasures of Dartmoor, from its 'wilderness' qualities to the delightful countryside on its borders.

I have not suggested how long they will take, because readers' walking abilities will vary greatly. You or a member of your party may be elderly, very young, ill or convalescent, or you may just have decided to take up walking and want to start modestly. I have not selected the walks with pushchair or wheelchair use in mind.

## Footwear

The range of surfaces you will meet on short Dartmoor walks is much the same as you would meet on long walks. Ideally therefore, wear walking boots – certainly not sandals! On most walks you will encounter at least one wet or muddy patch, and many more after a period of rain. Walking any distance in wellington boots is not recommended (they can damage your feet and even your spinal posture) but a single short walk of under 5 km shouldn't cause a problem for most people – except be careful not to twist an ankle, since wellingtons provide no support and the ground is often uneven.

## Maps

The sketch-maps in this book are just that – sketches. Anyone walking on the moor should use the Ordnance Survey's Dartmoor map, OL28.

## Safety

Dartmoor requires respect. Its north-west hills in particular attract low cloud. Within the cloud, visibility can be suddenly reduced to a few metres. It can be damp, chilly and disorientating. Even for a short walk on the high moor, I always carry a map and compass, as well as extra clothing including a waterproof.

Riverside walks should not be attempted if the river is in flood.

Some parts of the moor are used by the military and live firing takes place. The boundaries of the three 'ranges' are clearly marked by posts. Flags are flown on prominent tors when the range is in use. At weekends, peak holiday periods and on many other days the ranges are (generally) open to the public and they include some of the wildest parts of the moor. Details of the firing programme are available on a recorded message by phoning 0800 458 4864.

Do take care if you go with children that they know not to pick up any strange object – but I have yet to see anything of the kind.

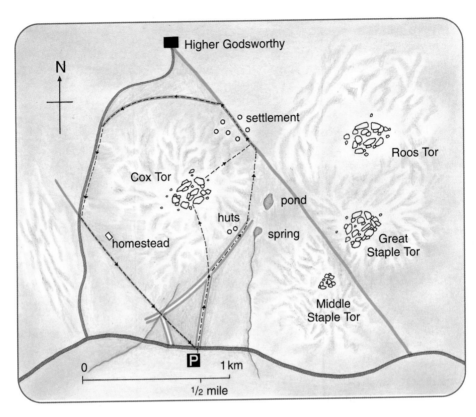

## Walk 1  Around Cox Tor

*Length: 4.8 km (3 miles)*
*Character: Beautiful open moorland (compass and map*
*recommended). Two versions of the walk are suggested. The one*
*including the ascent of Cox Tor is quite demanding, the other has a*
*steady climb. Particularly well drained grass to walk on, except up the*
*tor. There are many remains of prehistoric settlement around the hill,*
*but they are unobtrusive. Extensive and more easily visible remains of a*
*prehistoric village can be found north-west of Roos Tor and are visited*
*in Walk 2.*

*To get there: Take the Princetown road from Tavistock. There is a huge*
*car park about 200 m beyond the cattle grid at the entrance to the*
*moor, generally with an ice-cream van. (SX 532751).*

Cross the road from the car park and head due north to ascend the tor
(see opposite for the easier alternative). It is quite a stiff climb, but the
views are outstanding. The two tors to the east are Staple Tor (nearer

4

the road) and Roos Tor.

From the triangulation point on the summit, head down north-east, to the left of Roos Tor. You will reach a lightly used path running at right angles.

Turn left along this path, and you will begin to circle the tor.

The path will bring you out onto a tarmac lane, but you can walk beside it on the grass. After 700 m you will pass a disused quarry on the left; then after a further 350 m you bear left where indicated by discreet PUBLIC FOOTPATH signs. After 200 m, and 20 m to the left of the path, are the remains of a homestead, apparently prehistoric, though there seem to be some rectangular shaped humps which may suggest it is more recent. Continue on the broad track which follows the contour round the tor and brings you back to the car park.

*Easier alternative:* Instead of climbing the tor, take the track round its right side, which climbs at 10% rather than 25%. By the head of a stream, a lesser track bears off to the left. Follow this and when it soon peters out carry on circling around the tor. You should easily pick up the path; turn left along it and follow the instructions in the previous paragraph.

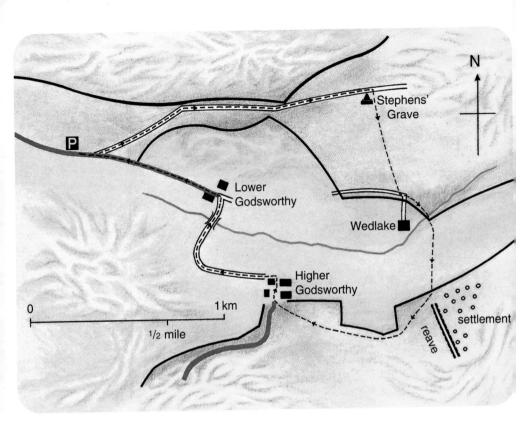

## Walk 2  Peter Tavy

*Length: 5 km (3¹/₄ miles)*
*Character: Beautiful scenery on the edge of the open moor, with a large Bronze Age settlement to explore.*

*To get there: Peter Tavy lies 3 km north of Tavistock on the A386. Turn right across Harford Bridge, then turn left into and through the village. Pass the church on your left; 100 m further on, turn right into a narrow lane. After 800 m, a disused quarry on the left serves as a car park (SX 522779).*

Turn left out of the car park, and after 100 m bear left up a stony track. After climbing steadily for 1.4 km you will reach Stephens' Grave: John Stephens of Peter Tavy committed suicide in 1762, apparently after being jilted, and was buried after the grisly fashion which religion in those days required, at this remote moorland crossroads.

Turn right here along a grassy track. When you reach a wall, turn left along it. Don't take the metalled track into Wedlake farm but continue along the wall.

6

*Passing the extensive remains of the Roos Tor settlement*

Descend to a stream and go through a gate (PUBLIC BRIDLEPATH); follow the signs. Just to your left as you leave the enclosure through a field gate is an extensive Bronze Age village which is well worth exploring – some 70 or more huts, so probably a town by the standards of 3500 years ago, and intriguingly they all lie to the east of a massively broad 'reave' or stone hedge. Return to the gateway.

From the gateway, you need to bear right towards the prominent corner of the enclosure walls, where there is a solitary diminutive hawthorn tree.

Follow the path along the uphill side of the enclosure wall. When the wall turns abruptly away, bear right along the lower path – towards Brent Tor if visibility allows you to see it! Join a tarmac lane which enters Higher Godsworthy by a cattle grid and thread your way through the farm complex (see map) and out along a metalled track which leads to Lower Godsworthy.

Here you turn left onto a tarmac lane which will lead you back to your car.

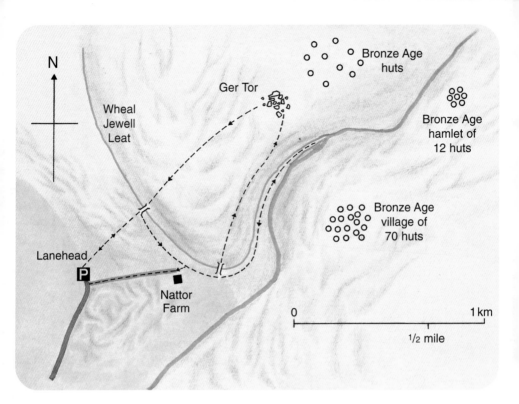

## Walk 3  Tavy Cleave

*Length: Each walk is approximately 3.5km (2 miles).*

*Character: Two walks for the price of one! Walk A is virtually flat, there-and-back. Walk B is circular and quite strenuous. Both venture into Dartmoor's most dramatic river valley. Wild and desolate though it may now seem, in the Bronze Age the surrounding hillsides were dotted with large and presumably prosperous settlements.*

*Access:  These walks are within the Willsworthy military range, which is the most used of the three Dartmoor ranges. An enormous red flag flies in the car park on firing days, so there is no risk that you won't know! Access is generally allowed throughout August, and at weekends, except for the weekend including the second Sunday in the month (presumably the padre could explain this). But it is worth phoning 0800 458 4868, where a recorded message will detail the planned firing days, because other non-firing days do occur.*

*To get there:  From Mary Tavy, follow the brown signs for the Elephant's Nest pub at Horndon, then follow signs for Willsworthy and then Lane End. There is a large car park (SX 537823).*

8

*Tavy Cleave, north Dartmoor's most dramatic valley*

Both walks: From the car park head for the prominent rocky hilltop ahead of you, which is Ger Tor. A well-beaten path leads from the flag-pole up a gentle slope to a leat: turn right along this side of the leat.

*Walk A:* Continue along the footpath this side of the leat, which curves round to go up the valley. You will reach a concrete sluice. Turn back here. On your return, you can take a short cut (see map).

*Walk B:* Walk along this side of the leat to the next concrete bridge. Cross this and take the path uphill. At the top of the first ridge you will get a magnificent view of Tavy Cleave and the surrounding hills. Now head for the top of Ger Tor! On a good day you will get extensive views; you should be able to see your car and the Willsworthy farms to the south-west.

There is a scattering of Bronze Age hut circles about 200 m to the north-west of Ger Tor, and you may want to explore these. You may also be able to trace the remains of ancient field walls, known as 'reaves'.

Find a route down through the clitter (scattered boulders) on the west side of the tor. Pick up a beaten path which becomes ever more distinct as it nears the leat and returns to the car park.

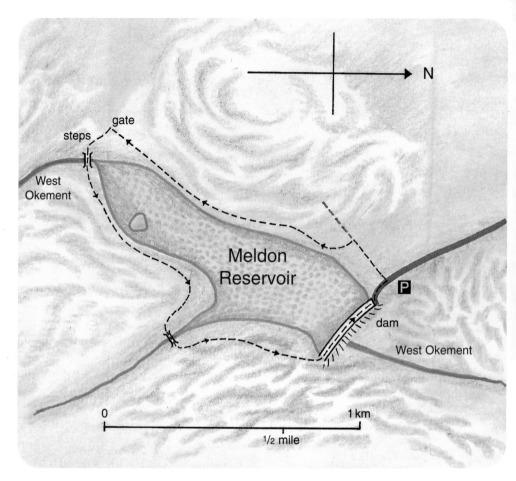

## Walk 4  Meldon Reservoir

*Length: 3.6 km (2¹/₄ miles)*
*Character: An easy and locally very popular walk, with two short
ascents and a steep descent by steps. Views up to high Dartmoor. The
walk lies entirely outside the military ranges. It is particularly fine
when the hawthorn is in blossom.*

*To get there: From the eastbound A30, turn left to the B3260 signed
OKEHAMPTON. (There is no comparable turn westbound, so you need
to go up to the A386 and return a short way along the eastbound
carriageway.) Turn right through Meldon village, then turn left and
left again into the reservoir car park at SX 562918.*

Leave the car park by the steps beside the toilet block. Cross the lane
and go through the gate (RESERVOIR WALK). After 100 m turn left and

10

follow a well beaten track for 1.3 km. Then go through a narrow gate and turn left down a track. Soon there is a flight of concrete steps on the left, which leads you down to a footbridge over the West Okement River. Turn left across the grass and pick up a path returning along the other side of the reservoir.

This path diverts a short way up a steep coombe, crossing the brook by a wooden bridge, and brings you to the dam. Cross the dam and take the lane back up to your car.

---

**Meldon Reservoir**

This is the most recent Dartmoor reservoir, constructed – despite major opposition – in 1970. Water, like china clay and granite, is a Dartmoor resource which generates local controversy.

---

**Meldon Viaduct**

One of the most spectacular railway features of the south-west, this viaduct was built in 1874 as part of the LSWR line from Okehampton to Plymouth. It rises 36 m above the West Okement River and can be crossed by walkers and cyclists: trains run from Okehampton Station to the east end of the viaduct.

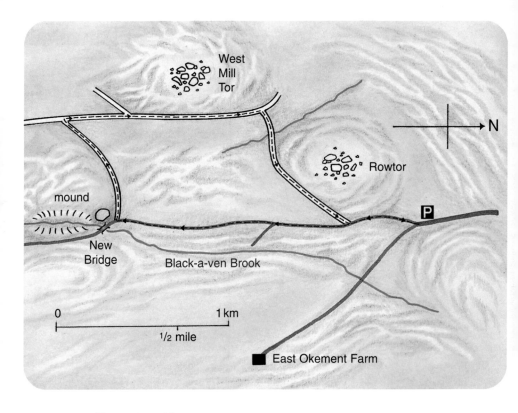

## Walk 5   East Okement

*Length: 5 km (3 miles)*
*Character: Wildest Dartmoor! This walk takes you into some of the
highest land in southern England – 500 m (1600 ft) above sea level –
with not a house to be seen, but it is relatively easy going, on dry tracks.*

*Safety: Low cloud is experienced as thick fog at this height, so you must
have a map and compass and extra clothing with you in case of a
sudden weather change. You will also enter the Okehampton Range,
where live ammunition is used in military training, so check before you
go by phoning 0800 458 4868, where a recorded message will detail the
planned firing days for Okehampton, Willsworthy and Merrivale
Ranges. Access is usually allowed at weekends and in the main tourist
months.*

*To get there: From Okehampton follow signs for OKEHAMPTON CAMP.
Keep to the left when you reach it, cross a cattle grid and a stream and
continue climbing the tarmac road till you reach a large parking area
on the right at a fork in the road (SX 596922).*

12

From the fork, take the tarmac road to the right. After 500 m keep left at another fork. Continue until you reach New Bridge, where there is a strange mound beside the road, and much evidence of tin streaming. The mound is the only undisturbed ground in the valley.

Don't cross the bridge, but retrace your steps for 80 m then turn left along a rough track for another 650 m till you come to a T-junction. Turn right. Pass West Mill Tor to your left. After 1km, turn right, cross a stream, and keep right (the main track), passing the military constructions just to your right.

The track gradually swings left to rejoin the tarmac track back to the car park.

---

### The military and the moor

The Army has been training on the moor for nearly 200 years, and in Victorian times there seem to have been annual camps for both regular forces and reserves. The permanent camp at Okehampton was established in the 1880s. An interesting account of the activities of the Victorian army can be found in William Crossing's *Dartmoor Worker* (Peninsula Press).

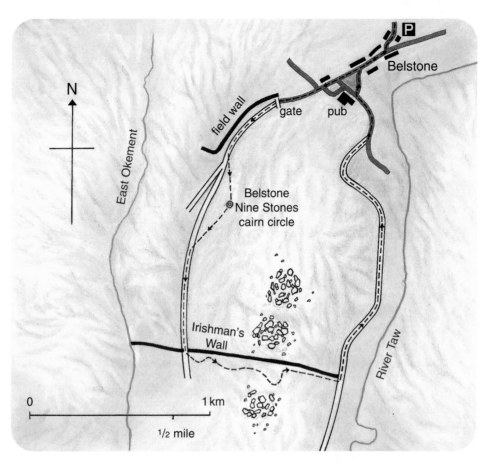

## Walk 6   Belstone Nine Stones and Irishman's Wall

*Length: 5.5 km (3¹/₂ miles)*

*Character: Quite tough going in places, over rough terrain, with one steep ascent and descent. Wonderful scenery, with a feel of the wild moor, and an interesting 'stone circle' – which is actually the remains of a burial cairn. The walk stops well short of the military firing range.*

*To get there: Take the Sticklepath road B3260 east from Okehampton, cross the A30 and take the second on the right to Belstone. Park in the main village car park (SX621939).*

Turn left out of the car park into the attractive village, keeping right at the stocks, and then right again to pass the 'telegraph office', immediately keeping left up the hill on the 'main' lane for 300 m. Pass the waterworks, go through the gate and follow the track until the wall on the right turns away from the track.

14

At this point a lesser track bears off to the right of the main track. Don't follow either of them! Instead, bear off 30° to the left of the main track (i.e. approximately 11 o'clock from it) heading towards a distant valley. After about 200 m you will see the Belstone Nine Stones. Now bear right, slightly downhill, to rejoin the track you were following. Keep to the main track.

After about 600m, and just before another track joins from the right, you will reach the ruins of a wall which crosses at right angles. It is very ruined, so not absolutely obvious. This is Irishman's Wall, said to have been built before 1810 as the northern boundary of a huge enclosure, which would have cut off Okehampton Commons from the moor. Okehampton's inhabitants went out at night and demolished it, after which the Irishman took the hint – or so 'tis said!

Turn left beside the wall, and climb to the top of the ridge ahead of you by whatever path you choose. (The ground to the right of the wall is a little less rocky than the direct route.)

Once at the top, use the view as an excuse for a breather, then make your way down the other side, again by whatever route you choose: take care, as it would be easy to turn an ankle. In summer there's usually a bracken-free path near the wall.

A track runs between the ridge and the serpentine twistings of the infant River Taw. Turn left along it. After about 1 km, pass through a gate and keep left along a tarmac lane to the village. At a fork turn right back to your car – unless of course you prefer to visit 'The Tors' pub first.

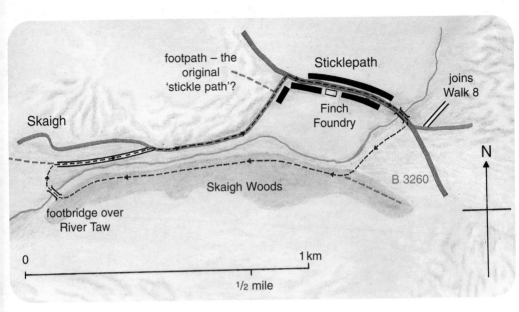

## Walk 7   Sticklepath and Skaigh Woods

*Length: 2.5 km (1¹/2 miles). Can easily be joined with Walk 8.*
*Character: Fairly flat, mainly easy but some uneven walking along*
*river bank. Interesting village, lovely woodland.*

*To get there: Sticklepath is on the B3260 east of Okehampton. Park in*
*the main street, somewhere near the Finch Foundry.*

Walk down the main street to the bridge, noticing the waterwheel at
Albany House. This is a modern wheel, but historically there were two
wheels working in tandem on this site, and a number of others within the village, all taking advantage of the free power of the River Taw.

Beyond the bridge turn right (PUBLIC BRIDLEPATH). Stay the same
side of the river, through a gate, then turn right (SKAIGH WOODS AND
SKAIGH). Follow the path through Skaigh Woods beside the rushing
stream, past rapids and a weir. You will reach and cross a footbridge.

---

### Sticklepath

The dialect word 'stickle' was an old Saxon word meaning steep
and difficult, when applied to paths. The Rule of St Benet stated
that 'The way is narrow and stickle that to Life and Heaven's riches
leads.' The riches in this particular Sticklepath came mainly from
copper mining and also from the numerous mills which lined the
village street.

---

16

The path bears right, up to a track. Turn right signed SKAIGH (unless you want a longer walk in which case explore the left turn to BEL-STONE). The track soon becomes a tarmac lane which emerges onto the B3260 at the top end of Sticklepath Village.

Just before it does so, a path to the left leads up to Greenhill, the site of a former copper mine. I suspect this path was the pre-turnpike route to Okehampton – the path originally described as 'stickle'.

---

**Finch Foundry**

This fascinating little factory was used from 1814 to 1960 to make edge tools, and is powered by three waterwheels. It is maintained by the National Trust, and demonstrations are given regularly during opening hours (seasonal). It is well worth a visit.

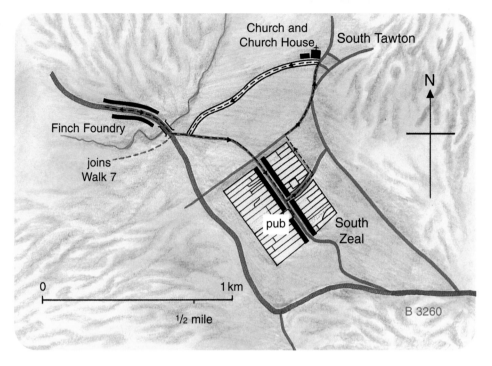

## Walk 8  South Zeal, South Tawton and Sticklepath

*Length: 3.6km (2¹/₄ miles). Can be joined with Walk 7.*
*Character: Easy walking, mostly on very quiet lanes. Explores three*
*villages of considerable historic character and interest.*

*To get there: Follow B3260 east from Okehampton to Sticklepath, then*
*just after the river bridge bear left to South Zeal. Go right down the*
*village street and park below the Oxenham Arms, an impressive*
*building, once a gentry house but now an attractive pub.*

Walk up to the medieval chapel of St Mary's and turn right, passing
the school. After approximately 200m turn left on a footpath, and
study the area of land between the path and the houses in the main
street. The long strips are 'burgage plots' (see box opposite).

   Walk past the backs of the burgage plots, cross a stile and turn right
along a lane. At the cross-stump, keep left into South Tawton. St
Andrew's church, the medieval church-house (dated 1572) and the
lych gate form a most attractive group.

   Take the bridleway signed TARKA TRAIL to the left of the church-
house. When after 1km you reach the tarmac lane, turn right, which
will bring you into the village of Sticklepath, home to the fascinating
Finch Foundry (see page 17).

18

Notice the toll house on the Sticklepath side of the bridge. The old road from Okehampton to Crockernwell ran through South Zeal – which was fine as long as there was no wheeeled traffic: even as late as 1788, a traveller took a whole day travelling by carriage from Lydford via Okehampton to Crockernwell – and did not see another wheeled vehicle the entire way, only trains of pack animals with panniers or yokes on their backs. At that time the main Okehampton-Exeter route was via Crediton. The turnpike road which forms the South Zeal by-pass probably dates from around 1800. It is a rather fine example of engineering, using the minimum construction work to create a relatively smooth gradient suitable for coaches.

From Sticklepath bridge, bear left along the lane into South Zeal.

---

**Burgage plots**

South Zeal was a medieval planned town. Each inhabitant of the new town purchased or rented a house on the street together with a long thin plot (at South Zeal one furlong deep) running back from the road. These were, and in some cases still seem to be, miniature farms. Many of the householders would have held additional land or common rights elsewhere, and they could develop a trade using their street frontage as a shop.

In successful towns of this kind, later streets were built parallel to the main street, across the line of the burgage plots, but South Zeal never got further than stage one of the plan.

---

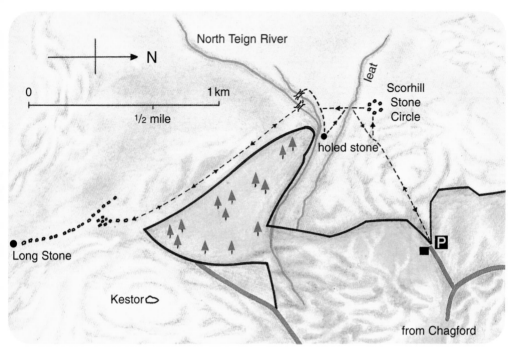

## Walk 9  Scorhill and Shovel Down

*Length: 5km (3¹/₄ miles) or 2.4km (1¹/₂ miles)*
*Character: This is a 'there-and-back' walk but of great interest, visiting some of the finest Dartmoor antiquities. You can choose between a very short stroll, and a longer one.*

*To get there: From Chagford market place, take Mill Street (past James Bowden's and the Bullers Arms) and bear right at the fork. Turn right at the crossroads and cross Chagford Bridge. Then turn left and follow signs to GIDLEIGH. Ignore the right turn to GIDLEIGH/CHAPPLE, then at the next junction keep left up a dead end to Scorhill where you can park (SX661877).*

A gate leads onto the moor. Follow the main track up towards the top of the hill ahead of you, then follow a path down. When it forks, bear right and in 200m you will reach the Scorhill stone circle.

Now aim for a point about 100m to the right of the nearest conifer plantation. You will cross a leat (artificial watercourse) and pick up an old track down to the ford, where you can cross using a clapper bridge, then a second.

(*For the short walk:* Don't cross the clappers, but turn left along the river bank. Miss out the next paragraph, and start again at the *.)

20

*The Scorhill stone circle is one of seven circles in an arc around the north-east edge of the moor*

Bear slightly left, and walk parallel to the plantation wall. After about 1 km, at the far end of the plantation, turn right uphill. Two stones standing nearly waist high mark the foot of the first of the Shovel Down stone rows. Most of the stones have been robbed out of this first row, but continue uphill and you'll find this 3500 year old religious site becomes more impressive. Explore the rows as far as you want – they end at a tall menhir – then return by the same route. When you have crossed the clappers, turn right along the river bank.

* After 100m you will find a strange holed stone by the river, more or less opposite the corner of the plantation. In former times this was thought to cure rickets, if the patient was passed through it.

Now head uphill, back towards the bridge over the leat, then down to your car. Note how animals can be funnelled towards the gate.

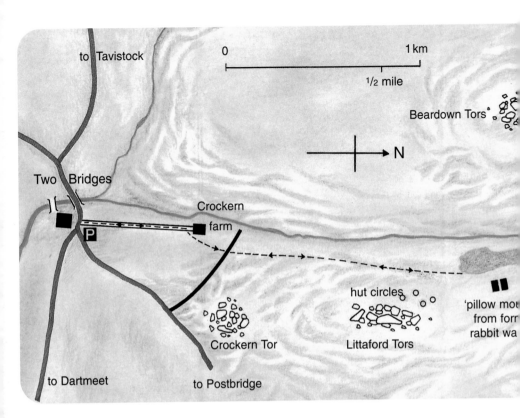

## Walk 10  Wistman's Wood

*Length: 4km (2¹/2 miles)*

*Character: A lovely walk out onto the open moor, to a fascinating piece of ancient woodland. This is a there-and-back walk, but I am certain you will not be disappointed.*

*To get there: The car park is directly opposite the Two Bridges Hotel, at the point where the two main roads across the moor, B3212 and B3357, briefly join forces. Park in the former quarry just to the north of the road (SX609750).*

Walk north through a gate and up a track to Crockern farmhouse. Keep to the right of the house, and follow the well used track along the side of the valley until you see Wistman's Wood ahead of you. There is a stile at the entrance to the nature reserve.

Information boards describe the significance of this wood of dwarf oaks, and their unique lichens, which are one of the few vestiges of the primeval woodland of Dartmoor. It was people, of course, who destroyed most of it – but for once the 21st century and global warming

*Wistman's Wood*

*Please don't venture within the wood itself: this environment is very precious and needs to be left undisturbed.*

*The name Wistman's is a reference to the Devil, who used to lurk near this spot (and perhaps still does) in the form of a huntsman with his hounds, ready to chase sinners into the wood, where the hounds would devour them. 'Wisht' is dialect for 'weird' or 'supernatural'*

are not responsible: the woodland clearances of Dartmoor began in the Mesolithic period 7000 years ago, and the destruction was virtually complete by 2000 BC.

As you return, you will be passing Crockern Tor on your left. This was the venue for the Stannary Parliament, an open-air meeting of the tinners of Dartmoor (those who owned the tin-works, not usually those who got their hands dirty) who had long-standing legal rights. They even contested the power of the Westminster Parliament within the Stannaries, going so far as to arrest an MP who objected to them silting up the River Plym. It is said that Sir Walter Raleigh, as Lord Warden of the Stannaries, presided at some of these meetings, which were held in the middle of the moor so as to inconvenience everyone equally!

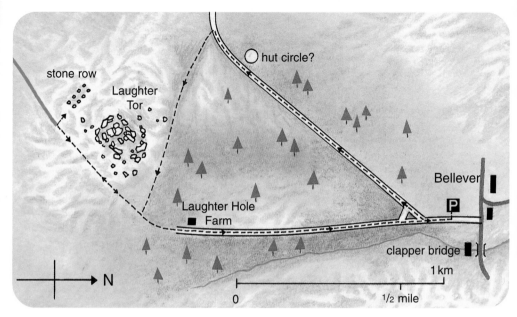

## Walk 11 Bellever Forest

*Length 3.7 km (2¹/₄ miles) or optionally 4.7 km (3 miles)*
*Character: Easy walking with a long but gentle ascent and descent,*
*partly through conifer forest, partly open moorland.*

*To get there: From Postbridge on the B3212, start heading towards*
*Princetown, then almost immediately turn left. On reaching a*
*T-junction in Bellever, turn left and after 100m turn right into a large*
*car park within the wood. Start the walk from the notice board on the*
*verandah of the public toilets – how many loos can boast a verandah?*
*(You could as an alternative take the Forestry Commission waymarked*
*walk of 4 km, which stays within the woodland.)*

Walk forward to the track and turn right, initially following the red-
striped waymarks. Turn right through the picnic area, through the
gate at the end and up the track ahead of you, still following the red
waymarks, and climb steadily to the edge of the plantation. Shortly
before you reach that point, there is a small clearing on the right con-
taining what may be the remains of a hut circle – though even the
experts are unsure.

When the track, with its waymarks, turns off to the right, you go
over a stile beside a field gate onto the moor. Turn left and keeping
close to the wall climb to the ridge of Laughter Tor, then continue
down the other side until a track crosses your route. Turn left to
BELLEVER unless you want to take the extension.

*The stone row which you can visit in the extended walk*

*When you return to your car, don't miss the short walk down to the river (picture), then turn left along the bank to see the remains of Bellever clapper bridge*

*Extension:* Turn right along the track for 450 m. This will bring you to a double stone row some 50 m to the right of the path, which should be visible even above the summer vegetation. Most of the stones have been robbed out, but originally it led to the longstone in the distance, over 160 m away. Now retrace your steps.

Taking the BELLEVER route, go through the gate and after 100m keep right down a rough track. At the foot of the slope go straight on through Laughter Hole Farm (signed to BELLEVER), from which a long straight track brings you back to the picnic area. Keep right and follow the waymarked track back to your car.

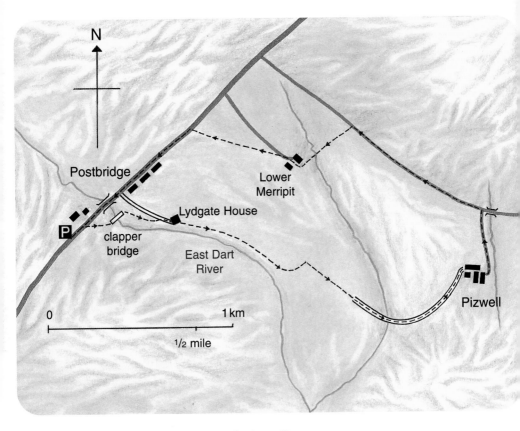

## Walk 12   Postbridge and Pizwell

*Length: 5.2 km (3¼ miles)*
*Character: Pleasant area of Dartmoor farmland. Easy walking but one spot can be very wet underfoot (and even overfoot!) after a period of heavy rain, when wellingtons might be better than walking boots.*

*To get there: Postbridge is on the B3212 between Moretonhampstead and Princetown. Park in the large car park near the National Park Information Point at Postbridge (SX 647789).*

Walk down to the bridges, and cross the medieval clapper bridge. Turn right along the bank and follow the PERMITTED PATH TO LYDGATE HOUSE. If this section is squelchy, you can expect to get your feet wet later in the walk.

The permitted path emerges onto a track. Turn right into and through the grounds of Lydgate House Hotel, which looks an enticing place to stay. Keep to the path which is clearly marked.

*The ancient clapper bridge stood on the post road from Exeter to Truro via Chagford. Wheeled traffic was unknown on Dartmoor till the 1780s*

From a field gate the path rises out of the valley, then turns sharp right. This path then joins a farm track, heavily rutted and likely to be muddy. When the hedges open out, keep right on the main track. Pass through a gate, then ford a stream: I have found the left side of the track the best option at this point, but neither is good.

When the track reaches a house, it bears left, goes through a gate and threads through Pizwell. This was one of the 'ancient tenements' of Dartmoor, whose existing rights to gather peat and wood were acknowledged when the moor was annexed as a Forest by the Norman kings.

Having followed the path through Pizwell, take the tarmac track out to the public road, where you turn left. After 700 m turn left, just before a bungalow, on the PUBLIC BRIDLEPATH TO POSTBRIDGE. Cross the ford (probably without getting your feet wet this time) and pass through a farmyard, along a tarmac track for 150 m, then keep left along a stony track.

On reaching the main road turn left, down to the river: but be careful along this road, where the traffic can be fast-moving.

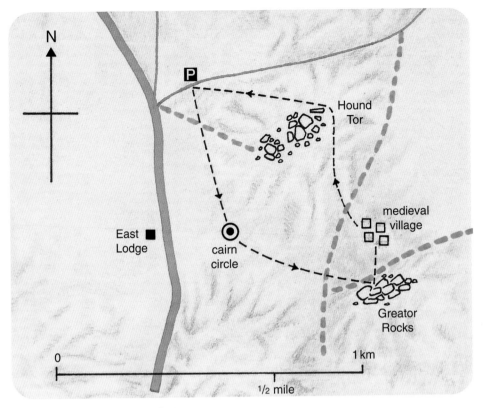

## Walk 13  Hound Tor

*Length: 2.6 km (1¹/2 miles)*

*Character: Hound Tor itself is popular with families, and the area is very beautiful (especially in May when it is covered in bluebells) but for me the main point of coming here is the medieval hamlet of eleven buildings, deserted some time in the 14th century, at or probably before the time of the Black Death, when the worsening climate made it impossible to grow corn and dry it.*

*To get there: From Widecombe, take the Bovey road B3387. Once over the top of the hill, turn sharp left signed HOUND TOR, then keep right. After 2 km (1¹/4 miles) there is a large and popular car park at Hound Tor, beside a fork in the road. A refreshment van – the 'Hound of the Basket Meals' (!) – is in frequent attendance.*

As you leave the car park, head to the right of the tor, about half way between the tor and the road. There are so many criss-crossing paths that it is impossible to give unambiguous directions. Look at the map, and you won't get seriously lost! The first point of interest is a cairn circle. The smaller stones, or perhaps earth, have all been removed,

*Greator Rocks*

*A general view of the medieval village, with Hound Tor in the background. Each house has one or two upper rooms for humans and a lower room for livestock – really cosy!*

leaving most of a ring of kerbstones, and in the middle the 'cist' or stone coffin in which a body was laid.

From the cairn, head towards Hay Tor – a strangely shaped double tor on the near horizon. As you crest the slope, a smaller and nearer outcrop comes in sight, down and to the left – Greator Rocks (see photo): take any path down to this tor. From the centre of the outcrop, head towards Hound Tor and you will find the medieval village.

From the village, climb towards Hound Tor then skirt around its right hand side, following paths through the bracken round the far side and back to the car park.

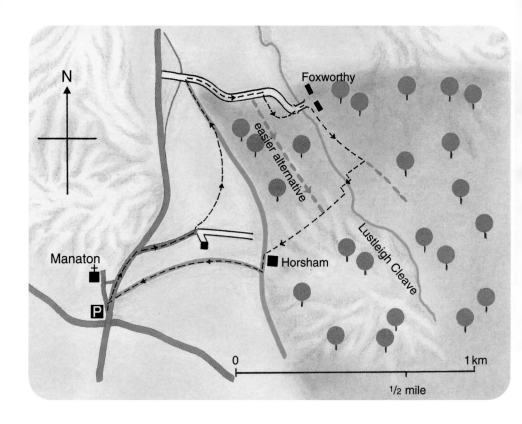

## Walk 14  Manaton and Foxworthy

*Length: 3.5 km (2¹/₄ miles)*
*Character: Short but strenuous. An extremely pretty, mainly woodland walk, with some farmland and a river of great character. Much of the walk is within a nature reserve. The return is steep enough to involve steps in places, and the river crossing requires considerable agility especially after rain (though it can be avoided entirely).*

*To get there: Manaton is north of Becky Falls, on the North Bovey road.*

From the entrance (not the exit) of the car park turn left, then take the right fork up the far side of the green and pass the village hall. 300 m beyond the hall, bear right on a tarmac drive signed as a dead end. After 270 m there is a junction and a cattle-grid. Take neither track. Instead, turn left through a field gate and down a footpath: after a few metres you enter a field.

 Cut across the middle of the field and through a gate. After a further 100 m, cross a stile into an English Nature reserve, and turn left along LANE TO FOXWORTHY.

*The beautiful hamlet of Foxworthy nestles at the bottom of a valley –
a classic Devon setting, far removed from the wild uplands to which
some of the other walks in this book will take you*

Descend through woodland. At a T-junction, turn right along a
concrete track. The hill on the other side of the valley is Hunters Tor,
which is surmounted by an Iron Age fort. At the foot of the valley,
turn right along a path (just before a gateway) which leads through
the wood to Foxworthy Bridge.

[For the alternative route, retrace your steps after taking in the
scene in the photograph, turn left up the concrete track, then left
again on a footpath through the wood (see map).]

Cross the bridge and turn right, signed HAMMERSLAKE etc. The
track becomes a path and enters woodland. Follow PATH signs. At a
junction turn right, PUBLIC FOOTPATH HORSHAM. Cross the stream
where you can – I found it best about 50 m downstream from the
point where you first meet the stream, but it's not easy anywhere.

Continue downstream on the other side; the path soon turns uphill
to the right, and becomes steep – very steep. Keep left, HORSHAM. Pass
a cottage, go through a gate and keep left (MANATON & WATER). then
right. By a shed/garage, turn right PUBLIC BRIDLEPATH MANATON. On
reaching the lane turn left back to the car park.

*An unexpected attraction within Yarner Wood is a disused mine which once employed 50 people, with the remains of a Cornish engine house half hidden by trees*

### Walk 15 Yarner Wood

*Length: Various trails are waymarked, so you can choose a walk – or walks – to suit your needs, from 1 to 6 km (³/₄ to 3¹/₂ miles).*

*Character: Part of a National Nature Reserve, much of it ancient woodland. A great place for bird-watchers but exuberant children might be out of place. At the time of writing, entry hours are 8.30 till 19.00 (or dusk if earlier). Dogs are allowed but only on leads. No entry fee or permit is required. A very useful descriptive leaflet is available, currently priced at £1, including a map of all the walk options.*

*To get there: From Bovey Tracey take the Haytor road B3387, then branch right signed MANATON. After 2 km (1¹/₄ miles) turn left into the reserve, and follow the signs to the small car park.*